Niobe and Other Poems

Niobe and Other Poems

AARON EVAN BAKER

RESOURCE *Publications* · Eugene, Oregon

NIOBE AND OTHER POEMS

Resource Publications
An Imprint of Wipf and Stock Publishers
199 W. 8th Ave., Suite 3
Eugene, OR 97401

www.wipfandstock.com

PAPERBACK ISBN: 979-8-3852-2465-4
HARDCOVER ISBN: 979-8-3852-2466-1
EBOOK ISBN: 979-8-3852-2467-8

In memory of Charles Fornara

Contents

Contents

Acknowledgments

The Journal of Formal Poetry for publishing *Sunt Aliquid Manes* (at http://journalformalpoetry.com/_archive/_pdfFiles/Spring%20 13.pdf);

David Fraser for publishing *Niobe* and *Enkidu* (at http://www.davidpfraser.ca/fridays-poems-2016.html);

3:00 AM Magazine for publishing *Assinaros* and *Banu Qurayza* (at http://www.3ammagazine.com/3am/assinaros-other-poems/

DREAM

The wind that drove the rank dark grass
Was cool, not chilly, and a sky of equal blue
Forever barred the storm.
                              I dreamt you spoke,
But dreaming like a rotted thread dissunders,
Flies until no snare of thought can catch it.

If I rejoin you on that temperate hill,
I may retrieve some vestige of your voice.
Will you answer my profoundest questions,
Or dilate on the luster of the day?
Will you whisper an amused indulgence
As, unbelieving, I await the end?

SUNT ALIQUID MANES

The dead are something, I have heard; but I
Could never make them speak. One day, I walked
Beyond the customary corner. There,
A black path through the stripped and sodden trees
Somehow compelled a thought of her, and I
Almost believed that she and not her absence
Walked with me.
                I have returned to say
It was not so—though I walked all that day.

ETERNAL RECURRENCE

Joy wants deep eternity--
But the sweaty heat of shame?
Must I unwind its day again
If joy in endless cycles came?

NEARING YOU

A dated plinth of kings,
White wreckage of a throne,
Put me in mind of you,
As mute as any stone.

A tremor in the muscles,
A popping of the bone,
And I am nearing you,
As mute as any stone.

Time clears the hectic table,
Time picks clean the bone,
And I am next to you,
As mute as any stone.

EARWAX

Something there is that doesn't love clean ears:
That loads the moist earwax in fragrant seams
And makes of dry a tickling, crystal feather.
I know that there's no winning, yet insert
My Papermate as deep as it will go—
Back . . . Forth . . . No, I'm not tired of earwax wars.
My neighbors on the bus all pull away;
No doubt they wish they'd taken other roads.

NIOBE

Her children, nine days dead:
A burr of blood's copper,
A sweeter sting of shit,
A darkest thrum of greening meat--
And her townsmen, turned to stone.

She ate, they say,
And lie who call this comfort:
This rote reduction,
The grinding of her teeth
And peristalsis of her bowels;
Merely a fated spasm
Before she turned to stone.

Here find our conclusion:
Seems dissipates like pyre-smoke,
Is greets us at rock-bottom.
No abatement, no release
Except one turn to stone.

THE SIREN

So long a voyage
To loiter in the surf?
Your every road—here.
You were rebuffed—
Each repulse her bait.
Bartók, Tallis,
Your off-key humming—
Each her music,
Beguilement and deliverance—here.

Up the beach, toward the rocks . . . .
No thirsty succubus,
But a Gorgon's face, itself stone.

DRUNKENNNESS

After the barlight soft on sweaty faces,
After the Bloody Mary,
After the Zinfandel,
After the Cabernet and the Maker's Mark,

And the ordinary jokes,
And then the Greek joke:

The Cannibal King said: The earth is round,
And the Greek Sailor said: Will you fuck me?

Both interpreting the same symbol--

Then it's out, out, out into the cool and rain,

The girl walking fast,
A cellphone glowing in her pocket,

The El a cannonade above you,

And you are headed homeward, more or less;

And this moment and this hour
Will wheel away
And wheel again,

World without end--

No more nor less
Than peerless Helen,
Or the ships at Mylae,
Or a wind in Nietzsche's hair --

As much as these,

This moment and this hour,

Snugged against the rain,
Waiting for the El.

Equal the words:
World without end
and
Will you fuck me?

SOMEWHAT AFTER EZRA POUND

What if at midnight in the black back yard,
peak of that pine is laced with a moon-snow cap?

And what if at midday,
a red ant's off to her wars?

Not her forefoot will save you--

not her ruddy foot,
nor daggered helm,
nor click of martial carapace;

nor the night-green shags,
nor finery imported from the moon

will save

you, bent on a human business
that you have badly done
and still must do.

ENKIDU

Bread and beer,
Emblems of the wild man's arrival.
He scrapes his face with copper,
Then drinks and eats too much.
His stubble is wet with vomit.

Observe the Temple Tower
(Its facing bright like copper!);
Hear a story of the wild man
Tamed--four beats to the measure;
Observe a swollen corpse
Bobbing on the swollen river.

We seek to know
Not so much how it was
As how it felt:
Closer to the edge of iron, bronze, or copper.

Sun chapped,
Ice bit,
Sickness nested in the bowels,
Copper split the skin—
All inescapable, a given there.

We seek but stumble, safe in our studies;
No knowledge here,
This comfortable supposing;

Safe so far--
Distant for now the edge
That finishes and defines,
That makes us matter
For another story.

ASSINAROS

Once, beaten men came to the river
To stage a fitting dénouement.
Some may have prayed: "Hide us oh Lord";
Some may have begged sweet drink
As needful children beg their mother;
Some may have blessed the kindly river,
Savior from thirst and feathered death,
As they went with their armor to the mud.

Students who heard that tragedy
Beside what may have been the river,
Conjectured what the author meant:
Guessed empire condignly punished,
Guessed no rebuke (all rule who can),
Or shelved grand themes and marked
A warning, so, should bad day come,
They'd stand clear while others drowned.

Sun for no reason danced with the river:
White fire, brown fire, blue;
A bird called, and a fat fly buzzed,
Suiting their purposes . . . .

Such beauty and indifference mastered me
Till, falling out with artifice,
I longed to scour the floodscape clean.

I thought:
We stand by a Sicilian river,
No brown god or slaking savior,
No tributary of our musings,
No end ordained by durant prose,
But a mute given, where men broke.

The bluff pronouncement almost worked:

I thought I looked on naked nature;
But I could not compel the river.
Like metals moving,
Facets of the flood-face wink and dash;
A bird cries;
Flies mob some ordure on the bank.
Men came and prayed, and a mud-slurred voice
Avows in full the tragedy.

BANU QURAYZAH

To stand aside,
To be left alone,
To live unnoticed--
All now too much.

A terrible simplifier comes.

To live—
Too much.

A terrible simplifier.

You speak
and stumble in the toils of speech.
Too much--
Now hear the predetermined answer.

Don't you see?
The summoner never stops
and none return.

You thought this bitterness had passed.
This bitterness will never pass.

Another,
and another,
and another comes.

PSALM

Did she who was sterile sing
When the urgent seer commanded?
And the prisoner drop his chain
When light and messenger descended?

Though flies pollute the altar,
Come thunder, come gray wing;
I'll fumble off the halter,
I promise I will sing.

HER DREAMING

It is this dreaming in the dark house kills;
Not the damp beat of fists on a wood floor,
Not fat tears in the attic, till attic fills
With tears, it seems—and then they break the door.

It is this dreaming wrecks the work of rage:
Rage wore out the rager, and she fell,
And didn't care to bluster at the cage
They offered—nearly forgot the bloomtide smell.

Once she had crushed in a fistful dripping cherry,
Bowed head to snuff the nectar in her palm,
Tossed the mashed petals for a make-do flurry,
Then wandered slowly in a craze of calm.

She could rage past all pain, if pain were all;
But she dreams of nectar, and a wild flower fall.

LOVE AND THE MATERIAL SOUL

(For Martha Nussbaum)

"Soul is no metaphysic mist; we know
Composure of the thoughtful, wantful mind,
The shaken branch of nerve, the heart-forced flow,
Bone, brawn, and skin--we grasp it, core and rind."
Two lovers posit solid truths that bind
All strands of sense; enrapt they richly move,
Tremble at touch of lips, of leaves, but find
No full requital in a finite love.
They want a truth contention cannot prove:
Soul not annulled, not a seed-husk, but new.
Hearing at early coffee the first dove,
Both wish a sign; composed, they look for you.
Birds call and quarrel in the wood till night;
Both feel the chill, consent to passing light.

DEFERRAL

Pain had changed her face;
She left him then and died.
One year before he knew;
They felt such grief should hide.

Grief did them one better:
He shrugged when he was told,
Deadbolted every exit,
Put everyone on hold.

But he could not stay hidden,
Letting the others shout;
Nine years force the issue;
Grief, like truth, will out.

And they confess surprise,
And murmur head to head,
To see him shake and keen,
Keen for the ten years dead.

THE MYSTIC

To him it seemed the sky must break,
Granting a message long delayed.
He waited, and began to shake;
"Just once, just now's enough," he prayed.

The sky was banal blue all day;
The tethered earth turned as it should;
His heart had sped. He'd not betray
The end unspoken, ill or good.

REPLY TO YEATS

It matters if you drink from impure ditches:
Ache, dysentery, cramp, fresh sores, and itches
Teach better than your high-note blarney can
The wounding, killing, stinking truth to man.

ASPIRATIONAL

We fight for trash, then stare (thug, cheat, and liar),
Mouths agape at heaven's punctual fire.

THE CAT

Her whining, dander, smells
Seemed hardy as Precambrian stone.

No clench
And muscular explosion (pounce or dash),
But lassitude made flesh—and only death
Could be more still.

WHO

Who will shuffle words for you and me,
My darling, when we're gone as gone can be?

FAILED NARCISSIST

My mirror, which I ponder every day,
Reflects a wound. I cannot look away.

EXCLUSUS AMATOR

I've waited at a corner you won't come to;
I've waited at a door that you won't open;
I've waited for an answer you won't utter;

I knew it was no good; I knew and waited.

Once was hope that words, my brassy heralds,
Would so confound reluctance with their timbre
That you would turn, elated by that music--
And then, amazed, you'd say the same to me.

Once was hope my poor implorators,
My words, troubled the air for; but the air
Remained just what it was before I spoke,
And you turned not at all, for all I spoke.

I knew it was no good; I knew, but waited;
And I will wait. Until my words are done,
Until I trouble nothing, I will wait.

CAESAR

One beats a slave to death for mealtime cheer;
One is a slave, and dreams a god of blows
To thunder justice till the good day come;

I stepped beyond. My promise to the pirates
Augured more than they could guess: I'd risk
All that man may, and win the sum of things.

To humble Gaul and Germany, or chase
A broken *princeps* to the southern Shore—
What need to calculate another's cost?

That done, what then? Head east like Alexander?
Or north to settle Germany's account?
Or play the reeky crowds at Rome their king?

A game turns tedious pursued too long.
My aim immovable, what need for more?
I shrugged and let the Spanish cohort go.

And those who killed me made me live, as I
Could not. So I won at the final hazard.

SPINOZA'S HEAVEN

If it were true that mind shall be forever,
Under the aspect of eternity--
The thoughtful attribute of all that is,
There freed from cause and consequence and time,
Freed and so forgetting all that's past—

I would not be forever, not forget
You and your smile when I played dinosaur,
Roaring to shake the prehistoric park--
Or how you scolded me and took me close
When I'd been lost (the neighbors brought me back)--
Or how pain made a shape I'd never seen
Of your dear face—and I asked what was wrong--
And you said you were sick—and then were gone.

No meeting in Spinoza's heaven then,
Freed of what made us dearest to each other--
For I would not forget you, forty years
Buried beneath the grass of Illinois.

VETERIS VESTIGIA FLAMMAE

This morning's warbler's three descending notes
took your attention as they'd once before,
and thirty years were nothing and you fell,

the old pain quite renewed--and the old hate:
chewing itself, it fed you well.

                             How could
she pain you still?

"She wants to dance with you," they said, and you,
only the latest project of her pity,
infatuate with hope, thought it was true.

Like a vagrant at a suburb window,
fumbling at the misted glass, you fell.

What did you see? For, neither beautiful
nor wise, she mastered you, not wanting to,
not wanting you.

                     But surely pain would tell:
she'd feel its weight and warp in you—such pain
on her account, she'd pity you again;
how could she put behind her so much pain?

No more. It is enough you fell.

                          Why should
she pain you still?

THE TORTURERS

One may conceive a similitude of hope
When patches of our filth are scoured away.
But surely those dishonorers must pay
If we're to reverence again that shape
And sovereign gesture that compelled the world?
Pay what can be paid—or we stay soiled.

ARISTONAUTES

He is now, as he was, at bay;
The stone has bodied his constraint.
Apart, forever poised to die,
He stands and masters his defeat.

I have studied how to die;
I know the limit of my reach;
But I can hope to seize that day,
To stand apart and not to flinch.

ASTRONOMICAL OBSERVATION

We are the sift of stars, and shall return
Whence we have come. Will you reject me then?
You will not care, I will not care, made one.
Only the pensive interval divides,
The aching interval. Go by, be done.

HOW TIRED I AM OF YOU

Punch to the head—career I should have had--
And you—my brain you see is rather bad.
Full stop, return—making the old pain new—
Full stop, return—how tired I am of you.

WHINGING

Whinging is whining with a tinge
Of the squealing of a hinge.

LUKKA

Talk of a strong man and his keep
Beyond Marassantiya's bend,
Of chariot dust that mars the sky
And ashwood spears anointed red,
Has reached this fractious land of Lukka.

Rumor of war,
Rumor of a kind of peace,
Even so far as Lukka.

But what is that to you and me,
This all in all and only you and me,
Our own law in our own sweet time,
Hotfoot or tangled on a sweaty bed
In this unruly march of Lukka?

The strong man conquers everywhere;
The gods must love strong men--
Even the fickle gods of Lukka.

We take no stock in gods,
Who dog our tracks with petty censure,
Then ratify successful murder--
Do keep the sacrifices burning!
We heard a tale: Love drives his cart
Over the feckless gods of Lukka.

Does he come this year?
Or must he mind his keep?
Perpend inquiring minds in Lukka.

Whatever comes, our plans abide:
We stray at will in our sweet time
On this uncharted and unchartered ground,
This unencumbered land of Lukka.

HOPE

Hope, the vampire, emptied me again
And then blew up—Leviathan of ticks
Or vast mosquito, crammed.
                                    And I, the rind,
Must . . . what? Endure? Try harder? Hold my breath?
Doubtless you know how I must meet my hurt;
But what if rind should seek to be itself:
Discarded scrap—food for the teeming dirt?

GREECE, 1986-1987

In the wreckage of a shrine whose gods
I might have greeted, I returned to laughter
And a field of goatshit, scrub, and stones.

These I recall in late, diminished days
From a year of seeming mastery.
These were enough—and in this iron age
Memory of these will armor me:
Your laughter and those tragic, goat-stained stones.

TRIFLE

I don't get over things too well;
And so I wish you still in hell.

REPRISE

Locus of your pity and disdain,
I speak for every disprized she or he.
Not that you asked--but I recall the pain:
Mirth and smiling welcome—and then me.

WHY

Why compound inveterate pain
And live off loss who might still gain?
The cure he hoped does not arrive,
And hatred proves that he's alive.

TUESDAY, 2:00 P.M.

To set the pens and pencils in a row
And pin mementos to the flaking board.
To shed one's dandruff, rub one's oily nose,
Abrade the itchy dermis of one's neck.
To scuff the carpet, cubicle to hall,
Then, thoughtlessly, come shuffle-stalking back.
To breathe, to sigh, to yawn, to simply be—
Ambition, chittering monkey, choked near dead,
For now unwanted and unwaited for.

DYSPHORIA

Weak now old man who wilded in my blood,
Undying itch with straying, sticky finger.
He'd genuflect to fist and groin—his grasp
Nowhere commensurate with his conceit.

Time was, tough customer, but now he's tame!
I sift volcanic sand and hope he's tame.

Better a eunuch—best, no man at all.

MISTRESS OF BEASTS

"She has delays," they said, although when pressed
they granted she would likely not arrive.

And I—who couldn't help, who couldn't start
to help, who couldn't think how I might start
to help—raged for a time, as one well versed
to kick at stones and tides and empty air.

Once she went to tend a neighbor's pets
and let me tag along. How calm and sure
each feeding, walking, stroking was! For she
was mistress though not cruel--and they
came sleekly to their ease, and never feared.

Your pardon, daughter, that I pitied you?
Wished you other than you must become?
For you, mistress of nature, eased my rage,
bound me to your service, bid me care
for every creeping, crying, wounded thing.

CONSISTENCY

No exaltation changes me.
What I was before the drunken hour
I am.